You're
NOT
Alone

You're NOT Alone

CARLA KNOWLTON

WestBow Press
PRESS
A DIVISION OF THOMAS NELSON

WestBow Press books may be ordered through
booksellers or by contacting:

WestBow Press
A Division of Thomas Nelson
1663 Liberty Drive
Bloomington, IN 47403
www.westbowpress.com
1-(866) 928-1240

Because of the dynamic nature of the Internet, any web addresses or
links contained in this book may have changed since publication and
may no longer be valid. The views expressed in this work are solely those
of the author and do not necessarily reflect the views of the publisher,
and the publisher hereby disclaims any responsibility for them.

Certain stock imagery © Thinkstock.
Any people depicted in stock imagery provided by Thinkstock are models,
and such images are being used for illustrative purposes only.

Scripture taken from the King James Version of the Bible.

ISBN: 978-1-4497-8325-9 (sc)

Library of Congress Control Number: 2013901593

Printed in the United States of America

WestBow Press rev. date: 2/12/2013

This book is dedicated to my two biggest sources of support, my husband and my mother. They are always in my corner, loving me, even when I am completely unlovable. They are my sources of gentle criticism and fierce devotion.

To my husband… Thank you for walking this journey with me. What a journey it's been! When I was bound by fear and doubt, you encouraged me, and reminded me that it's not about me after all. You have supported me and grounded me, even while persuading me to spread my wings and fly.

To my mother… Thank you for being my cheering section! Since my childhood, you have called me "Miss Wings." You make me believe I can do anything, and seeing the pride you have in me makes me strive to be better, to do better.

TABLE OF CONTENTS

INTRODUCTION

We often hear that we, as Christians, cannot go by our feelings. Our feelings, or our emotions, come from our hearts. Jeremiah 17:9 says, "The heart is deceitful above all things, and desperately wicked: who can know it?" The deeper our understanding of this fact, the more equipped we are to recognize and triumph over one of the most effective weapons in our enemy's arsenal.

The reality, however, is that as long as our heart continues its thud-thump cadence within us, we will be vulnerable to Satan's tactics. Our battle plan, therefore, is not to defeat our emotions, but to recognize how Satan uses them against us, and to learn how to defend ourselves, utilizing the armor God has specified for us.

As we journey with Christ, our emotions can often overwhelm us. We may experience criticism from others, fall prey to condemnation when we sense that we do not measure up to God's standards (or even our own), and may even be ostracized by the church or Christian community. The results can be tragic – we conclude that there is something wrong with us and we must strengthen our determination, or else we deem ourselves powerless and incapable, and deteriorate until there is nothing left of the spiritual life we once led, all the while wondering what caused this downhill slide in the first place.

So what hope do we have? Is there help? What weaponry is at our disposal? As well, how should we react when these feelings seem to overtake us? Is there anyone we can look to as our example?

As you read this book, I encourage you to look up each scripture in your own Bible. Do not merely take my word for it, but "Study to shew thyself approved unto God, a workman that needeth not to be ashamed, rightly dividing the word of truth." (2 Timothy 2:15) Earnestly seek the Lord God, ask Him to reveal the deeper mysteries of His Word, and allow Him to strengthen, encourage, and transform you according to His perfect will.

1

Your Primary Weapon

2 Corinthians 10:2-3 states, "For though we walk in the flesh, we do not war after the flesh: For the weapons of our warfare are not carnal, but mighty through God to the pulling down of strong holds." Without question, the most important – and the most powerful – weapon in our arsenal is also the most underestimated.

- 1 Corinthians 1:18 – For the preaching of the <u>cross</u> is to them that perish foolishness; but unto us which are saved it is the <u>power</u> of God.
- Ephesians 1:19 – And what is the exceeding greatness of His <u>power</u> to us-ward who believe, according to the working of His <u>mighty power</u>.

- Romans 1:16-17 – For I am not ashamed of the <u>Gospel of Christ</u>: for it is the <u>power</u> of God unto salvation to everyone who believes; to the Jew first, and also to the Greek. For therein is the righteousness of God revealed from faith to faith: as it is written, The just shall live by faith.

Are you starting to see it? The power of God lies in the cross of Christ.

Think back to when you first came to know Jesus Christ personally as your Savior and Lord. There came a day when you started to feel conviction. It was not Jesus' sinless life that drew you, nor was it His resurrection. It was the understanding that He died for you, that He gave His life as a ransom in order to open the door to a relationship with the Father. All who are saved have come to the cross of Christ, recognizing what He there did for us, and accepting His sacrifice into our hearts.

However, many of us do not realize that the blood Christ shed was not only for our salvation, but also for our victory, in every area of life. The blood of Christ broke the hold that Satan had over us. Because of sin, Satan had a legal right to each of us. When Christ died on Calvary's hill, the blood of that Perfect Lamb paid the legal debt that we owed. This means that Satan no longer had a claim to us, neither in the salvation of our souls or in the victorious life that we desire to live. This understanding allows us to access our most effective weapon – the power of God working on our behalf.

In the preface, we saw the commonplace results of Satan's mind games. When we understand how to access the power of God, the scenario plays out a little differently. That old serpent presents us with a bundle of feelings that begin to overwhelm us. We now know that feelings and emotions come from a wicked, deceitful heart, so our first reaction is to take those feelings to God in prayer. In doing so, we come to recognize the tactic of our enemy before it can be successful. We seek the Lord's help, believing that "The Lord is near unto all them who call upon Him, to all who call upon Him in truth" (Psalm 145:18). Then, as we patiently rest on God's promise, we become "…

renewed in the spirit of your mind" (Romans 4:23). We can accomplish this renewal by replacing our thoughts and feelings with what God's Word declares.

The primary method of "renewing our minds" is by daily prayer and Bible study. However, when the attack comes, it is also helpful to recognize others that have gone through the same battle. Having an example to follow is detrimental to guard against feelings of not measuring up, being too "messed up," or simply feeling alone. Learning from their experiences enables us to increase strength, to learn from their mistakes, and ultimately to win the battle.

The rest of this book will offer insights to many of the role models that the Bible bestows on us. The Bible presents many men and women as examples, but too often, we only know the Sunday school lessons we learned as children. We applaud these great men and women of faith, too often overlooking their struggles, doubts, and fears. Identifying the same human traits in them that we see in ourselves can greatly equip us in our own battles.

As you read, take time to meditate on each person. Give the Lord time to illustrate the distinct feelings of each, and times that Satan has used the same scheme on you. Allow God to encourage you as you discover how He was ultimately able to use each man and woman for His glory.

Gideon:
An Example of
Inadequacy and Unbelief

THE STRUGGLE

Have you ever felt reluctant to trust God? It is a common struggle among Christians, yet one that we seldom verbally acknowledge. What child of God wants to admit that they are having a hard time trusting God? Does that not sound like an oxymoron? Hebrews 11:1, 6 tells us, "Now faith is the substance of things hoped for, the evidence of things not seen...But without faith it is impossible to please God, for he who comes to God must believe that He is, and that He is a rewarder of those who diligently seek him." Why would we confess to others that our faith is weak and dimming?

Have you experienced feelings of inadequacy or unworthiness? Two common viewpoints exist – to be humble before God, and to know your worth. One side of the coin is taught behind the pulpit, and deals with who God is - the One who created everything we see; the One who cursed Egypt with plagues; the One who rains down fire and hail from heaven; the One who sits on the throne and judges mankind. Surely, this God demands fear and reverence. The other side of this coin we learn by the actions of others towards us, and deals with who we are. The wealthy acquire seats of prominence in the church; the well-educated are promoted to positions of authority; the leaders justify themselves and rarely admit to fault or weakness.

The truth lies somewhere in the middle, but are we really ever taught that truth? Do we habitually see it in action? With all that we encounter, both from the world and the church, it is easy to feel unworthy to stand before a holy God. We see ourselves as inadequate to do His will. The resulting confusion births within us a distrust of God.

THE STORY
JUDGES 6 & 7

The Israelites had been under great oppression for seven years. The Midianites continually destroyed Israel's land, ransacked their crops, and slaughtered their animals. This left the Israelites in severe poverty. Many of them were hiding in dens and caves out of fear.

The story narrows to one Israelite in particular, Gideon, the son of Joash. Gideon was threshing wheat by the wine press in order to hide the precious grain from the Midianites. The angel of the Lord appeared to Gideon and blessed him, saying, "The Lord is with you, you mighty man of valour." Gideon's immediate response revealed his distrust of the Lord. The Lord then told Gideon that he would save Israel from the Midianites' oppression. The next words Gideon spoke portrayed his feelings of inadequacy. All of Israel was poor, but his family was one of the poorest, and he was the least in his family.

Gideon then asked for three signs, and the Lord granted them. Each request helped to strengthen his trust in God, driving out by degrees Gideon's own feelings of inadequacy.

THE RELEVANCE

We, as spiritual Israel, are always under severe oppression from the world. Media bombards us with how we are to look, speak, dress, and think. "The American Dream" has become synonymous with "Keeping up with the Joneses."

The church does not provide much refuge. We no longer dress to look our best in the Lord's house on Sunday morning – we dress to outdo and impress one another. We give offerings in order to gain recognition, or so we can have a say in how the church spends its money. We hold positions in the church – not because of a calling God has given us, but because it looks good on our "spiritual résumé."

In Gideon's story, it is interesting to note that God did not send an outsider to deliver Israel. He chose one who was in the middle of the oppression. When God searched through all the Israelites, I can imagine several reasons why Gideon captured His attention:

1. Gideon was, so to speak, the poorest of the poor. Yet God did not find him with his hand out, expecting others to pull him out of this poverty. He was working, doing what he could to support himself and his family.

2. Gideon did not trust in God. He found it hard to believe all he had heard about this good, miracle-working God, since He had not done anything to deliver Israel out of the bondage of the Midianites. He felt forsaken and abandoned. Yet when the Lord appeared on the scene, Gideon was, at least, open-minded. He did not immediately trust God, but he did act in obedience, giving God a chance to prove Himself.

3. Gideon's feelings of inadequacy are apparent. The angel of the Lord calls him "a mighty man of valour." The word "mighty" in the original Hebrew is *gibbor*, meaning "powerful." The word "valour" is *chayil*,

meaning "a force, whether of men, means, or other resources". In essence, the Lord is telling Gideon that he is a powerful man of great resources. This was definitely not how Gideon thought of himself, given his present circumstances! Yet, he was willing to take his eyes off his circumstances and his own feelings long enough to listen to what the angel of the Lord had to say about him. He did not have to feel the same way about himself; he simply had to follow what the Lord said.

One of Satan's greatest strategies is to turn our eyes off God and onto ourselves. When we look at our lives, we see circumstances and situations that seem impossible to conquer. We may have a desire to do great things for the Lord, but our view sees only our own inadequacies, failures, and lack.

Given this, how can you defeat the enemy's ploy? How can you overcome your deceitful heart and its feelings?

The natural tendency is to believe that you will indeed do great things for the Lord once you have sufficient finances, know the right people, or increase your skills and abilities. However, God is a God of right now. He chose Gideon in spite of his "right-now" circumstances. God proves His riches by working through the lives of the poor; He proves His abilities by using the incapable.

As previously stated, your primary weapon is the cross of Christ. The blood that Jesus shed on the cross freed us from every hold Satan had over us. We no longer are bound by our past sins or our present circumstances. Satan's way leads to poverty, sickness, and death. God's way leads to blessing, health, and life. It is up to you to determine which way to claim for yourself. Your faith must ever be in Christ, and the victory and freedom that His blood bought for you.

Making this decision does not mean that your circumstances will automatically change and life will be easy from this moment forward. Our country may have missiles, but that does not stop enemy countries from declaring war on us. To the contrary, the cross has been Christians' primary weapon since Christ's blood first trickled down. The problem, however, is that we are rarely, if ever, taught how to use this weapon. A rocket launcher, no matter how powerful, is useless if you do not know how to use it.

The next obvious question would be how to "use" the cross of Christ to our advantage. Think back to when you were first saved. The only requirement was to believe. You did not have visible proof of what Jesus did for you on Calvary. You did not kneel at the altar and present to God your list of abilities or self-worth. You heard, in one way or another, the Word of God, which told you of what Jesus did for you, and you simply made the choice to take Him at His Word.

The way you were saved is the same way you are able to access the abundant life that He desires for you. Romans 10:9 says, "That if you shall confess with your mouth the Lord Jesus, and shall believe in your heart that God has raised Him from the dead, you shall be saved." We read in John 8:32, "And you shall know the truth, and the truth shall make you free."

Let us look again at Gideon. When the angel of the Lord first appeared, Gideon spoke with sarcasm. He found the angel's words hard to believe. If God was with him, then why was Israel under so much oppression? How could God use him, the youngest member of the poorest family, to deliver Israel? First, he asked for a sign that would prove who spoke with him. Look again at Hebrews 11:6 – "But without faith it is impossible to please God, for he who comes to God *must believe that He is*, and that He is a rewarder of those who diligently seek him" (emphasis added). You cannot believe the Word of the Lord until you believe it is really the Lord speaking to you. Whether the Lord's voice comes to you through listening to a sermon, reading the Bible, or during your personal prayer time, you must believe that it is the Word of the Lord. Gideon received a sign, and it bolstered his faith in God. It also gave him a sense of fear. In the presence of a holy and righteous God, our weaknesses and failures become more evident than ever. Gideon was not chosen because of his merit; in fact, no one is. The Lord told

Gideon not to fear, because he would not die. Gideon took the Lord at His word. He built an altar and named it Jehovah-Shalom, which means, "The Lord is peace."

That same night, God instructed Gideon to destroy his father's altar to Baal, build an altar to the Lord in its place, and sacrifice his father's bullock. Gideon was afraid of how his father and the men of the city would react, yet he obeyed the word of the Lord. The next morning, the men of the city were angry and desired to kill Gideon for what he had done, but his father intervened. Knowing the word of the Lord does not mean we will no longer have conflicting feelings. Now that your faith is exclusively in Christ and the cross, Satan will attempt to call your bluff. If he places fear on you, will you weaken your resolve? If he turns your attention to your inadequacies, will you admit defeat? You must stand firm, and know the Word of the Lord. God told Gideon that He would be with him. Gideon had a choice – would he believe his feelings, or the Word of the Lord? On a daily basis, you and I have the same choice.

Gideon now knew that the Lord was with him, and he knew His word. In essence, he tells God, "You gave me a sign to strengthen my faith in You. Now I'm asking for a sign that You will deliver Israel by my hand, to strengthen my faith in Your Word." God gave the sign that Gideon asked for. Mark 8:12 says, "And He (Jesus) sighed deeply in His Spirit, and said, Why does this generation seek after a sign? Verily I say unto you, There shall no sign be given unto this generation." If our desire is simply to receive a sign from the Lord, then we will not receive it. However, if our desire is to know Him, His Word, and His ways, then He will frequently confirm His Word in some way. He knows the intentions of our hearts, and desires to strengthen our faith in Him and His Word.

God had proven Himself and His Word to Gideon, and Gideon was willing to be obedient to what God commanded. Yet Gideon still struggled with fear. The Lord knew this, and provided another opportunity to fortify Gideon's strength. Gideon overheard two men talking. The first relayed a dream; the second interpreted the dream to mean that the Lord had already delivered Midian into the hand of Gideon. Matthew 6:8 reads, "…For your Father knows what things you have need of, before you ask Him." The Lord knows when we are weak and need added strength. He does not ask us to be strong on our own. He asks us to trust Him, and to be obedient to His leading.

We see in Romans 3:23 that "All have sinned, and come short of the glory of God." Not one of us is worthy or adequate. Still, we cannot let our feelings hinder us. The next time the enemy attacks with these weapons, remember that the blood Jesus shed at Calvary gives you victory from Satan and freedom from the bondage of your emotions. Prayerfully seek the Word of the Lord. Begin speaking the promises of God over your life and your circumstances. Stand firm, understanding that the enemy will come to test you. While you wait, look to that "great cloud of witnesses" (Hebrews 12:1) and learn from Gideon's example.

3

Elijah:
Ever Feel Alone
in Serving the Lord?

THE STRUGGLE

A vast number of United States citizens claim to be Christian. The quantity of churches dotting our country should attest to this. However, when we compare the meaning of the term "Christian" with the lifestyle of the average American, skepticism rises. The word "Christian" in the original Greek is *Christianos*, and means "follower of Christ." Acts 11:26 tells us that this term was first given to the disciples in Antioch. The disciples had been with Jesus. They lived with Him, ate with Him, talked with Him. They had spent so much time with

Him that they began to talk like Him and to act like Him. They began to be like Christ. Those living in Antioch noticed, and gave them the name "Christian."

Perhaps you have a younger brother or sister. Think back to your childhood and teenage years. How often did your younger sibling frustrate you by tagging along wherever you went, or by trying to mimic everything you did? In the human sense, it can be irritating, yet that is how we are to follow Christ. He yearns for us to tag along wherever He goes, and to mimic everything He does. That is the connotation of the word "Christian."

Millions of people today claim to be Christian; however, would the people of Antioch brand them as such? Is their lifestyle so different from the typical citizen, and so similar to Christ's, that the local townspeople would notice and label them?

At times, the Lord will turn the spotlight on us, allowing us to see ourselves through His eyes. We become aware of inconsistencies in our lives, areas where we are not lining up with His words. If we truly have a heart after

Him, then we desire to change, to be more like Him. Yet the enemy will often choose that time to attack. His weapon of choice is to turn our eyes to the world, even to the church, around us. We have an innate desire to fit in. The Lord may urge you not to partake of gossip; however, what would old Mrs. Bitty think if you refused to listen to the latest tidbit about Deacon Myer on Sunday morning? Perhaps you have a desire to witness to your co-workers; nonetheless, the inevitability of the nickname "Holy Roller" prevents you.

THE STORY
1 KINGS 18:17-39; 19:1-18

In obedience to the word of the Lord, Elijah met with Ahab, the ungodly king over Israel. Elijah called a meeting with all of Israel, 450 prophets of Baal, and 400 prophets of Asherah. Once assembled, Elijah reprimanded the people, asking how long they would waver between following the Lord God and following Baal. Elijah stressed that he, as the only prophet of the Lord present, would face the 450 prophets of Baal, and he challenged them to a test. They would each sacrifice a bullock, laying it on wood, but would not put fire to it. The God that answered by fire would be God to the Israelites. Everyone agreed, and the prophets of Baal prepared their sacrifice. They killed the bullock and laid it on the wood. They cried out to Baal, leaped on the altar, and cut themselves, but Baal did not answer.

Next, it was Elijah's turn. He sacrificed the bullock and laid it on the wood. He had men pour twelve barrels of water on the wood and bullock. Elijah then prayed, and asked the Lord to prove that He alone was God, and that Elijah had done these things at His command. Fire fell and consumed the wood, the stones, and the dust, and licked up the water. Upon seeing this, all the people worshipped and said, "The Lord, He is the God."

When Jezebel heard all that Elijah had done, she threatened to kill him. Elijah, afraid for his life, fled to the wilderness, sat under a tree, and began to pray. He asked the Lord to take his life. After lodging in a cave, the Lord asked Elijah what he was doing there. Elijah replied by listing what the Israelites had done, concluding that he was the only one left that served God. The Lord told Elijah to stand on the mountain. The Lord passed by Elijah, and a strong wind rent the mountain and broke it in pieces. There was then an earthquake, followed by a fire. The Lord was not in the wind, the earthquake, or the fire, but was in the still small voice that followed. The Lord again asked Elijah what he was doing there, and Elijah repeated his response. The Lord then tells Elijah to go to Damascus and anoint Hazael, Jehu, and Elisha. He then informs Elijah that He has a remnant of seven thousand in Israel that remained faithful to Him.

THE RELEVANCE

When we read the story of Elijah, we come away with a sense of awe at his dedication to the Lord. He was willing to stand alone before the false prophets and all of Israel. How steadfast, how courageous he seems! Yet to get a full picture of Elijah, we need to look to his earlier years. Elijah is first mentioned in 1 Kings 17. The first thing we see is the Lord instructing Elijah to leave his home and family and to hide himself by the brook Cherith. He was to be fed by ravens and to drink from the brook, and would remain there for two years.

What reservations must Elijah have had? What fears, doubts, and concerns rose in his mind? The scripture says that Elijah *hid himself* by the brook. That indicates that he had no contact with others. He did not dwell with others, build a house, or farm for his food. He was to be dependent on the Lord for his substance. After a time, I imagine he grew tired of eating the same food every day. The children of Israel had complained of the same thing in the wilderness when the Lord fed them manna. After a time, as Elijah noticed the water of the brook becoming dry, did he begin to worry? He must have also been quite lonely during so much solitude.

In order to develop such dedication for the Lord, the first requirement is time alone with Him. The Lord may not require each of us to "hide" ourselves. Yet He does command us to separate ourselves. 2 Corinthians 6:17 says, "Wherefore come out from among them, and be ye separate, saith the Lord, and touch not the unclean thing; and I will receive you." We are taught to be in the world, yet not of the world. We have daily contact with those in our family, church, school, and job. It is easy for those around us to influence our thinking and our behavior. However, we are to be separate from them; we must not allow ourselves to be swayed.

We learn to become separate during our time alone with the Lord. We may not be instructed to hide ourselves, but He does instruct us to study the Scriptures, that we can know His ways. He instructs us to pray without ceasing, that we may hear from the Lord. During these times alone with the Lord, He teaches us, strengthens us, and changes us. We often do not recognize the process as it is happening. However, there comes a day when we are able to look back and see what the Lord has done in us. We see how He has been maturing us, and proving His faithfulness.

As Elijah stood before Ahab, the false prophets, and the children of Israel, he could look back over the past few years and see God's faithfulness. Elijah had spent two years alone, learning to depend on the Lord for his sustenance. He had lived with the widow for a year, watching as the oil and meal were incredibly sustained, day after day. He had experienced the widow's son dying, and the Lord miraculously bringing him back to life.

It would have been much easier for Elijah to look the other way. He loved the Lord, and did his best to live according to His standards, but who was he to rebuke the king of Israel? Would the prophets of Baal try to harm him for insulting them and their god? What would the children of Israel think of him after he pointed out their hypocrisy?

God had called Elijah. Now Elijah had to make a choice. Which did he value most – the opinion of man, or the opinion of God?

You and I face that same choice on a regular basis. Matthew 10:37 says, "He that loveth father or mother more than me is not worthy of me: and he that loveth son or daughter more than me is not worthy of me." If we let our love for others interfere with our love for the Lord, then we are not worthy of Him. If we *truly* love the Lord, then we will keep His commandments (see John 14:15). If we *truly* love our friends and family, we will be willing to show them the truth of God's Word, despite the possibility of rejection.

This segment of Elijah's story has a successful end. Because of Elijah's obedience and faith, the Lord proved Himself. The children of Israel turned back to the Lord, acknowledging Him as the one true God.

Soon after, however, Elijah learned that his life was in danger. He fled in fear and complained, asking the Lord to take his life. Here we see a different side of Elijah. He no longer exhibits the boldness and faith that he demonstrated while challenging the false prophets of Baal. What caused such a dramatic transformation?

We gain insight from Elijah's response to the Lord. Elijah gave God a record of what the Israelites had done. We as Christians are quick to find fault in others, yet we rarely see our own. Elijah feared for his life, displaying a lack of trust in the Lord's protection. He fled to the wilderness, without seeking the Lord's counsel. He told the Lord that he had been very jealous for Him, meaning he had faithfully served Him, while cataloging the sins of the Israelites.

Have you ever been in that position? You are doing everything you can to serve the Lord and to live by His commands. You strive daily for maturity and greater intimacy. However, it seems like the closer you get to the Lord, the farther from Him everyone else becomes. Others begin to tease or outright degrade you for being over-enthusiastic. Sadly, much of this reproach comes from the church. Remember, Israel was the "church." They were God's chosen people. Yet they teetered between obedience and disobedience. Currently, the majority of the church does the same.

Sitting outside at night, the dark does not seem that dark. You are still able to see what is around you, and are able to walk around. However, the darkness of night seems extremely dark if you are sitting inside with the lights turned on. God is light (see John 1:4-9; 8:12; 12:46). The closer we get to Him, the brighter His light becomes in us. This makes it easier for us to recognize darkness in others, and hopefully in ourselves as well. This truth, however, does not give us license to judge others or to consistently point out their shortcomings.

Conversely, after being in the darkness for a time, coming into light is uncomfortable. The brightness of the light burns our eyes, making it difficult to see clearly. Similarly, those who are in spiritual darkness are often uncomfortable around us. Our commitment to the Lord increases our light, which in turn can negatively affect others. It presents them with a decision – turn away from the light and choose to remain in darkness, or allow the light to penetrate and change them. John 3:20-21 says, "For every one that doeth evil hateth the light, neither cometh to the light, lest his deeds should be reproved. But he that doeth truth cometh to the light, that his deeds may be made manifest, that they are wrought in God." Regrettably, many choose to remain in darkness rather than be changed.

The next time you feel alone in serving the Lord, pray that He will show you His remnant, that He will place in your path others that are unmovable in their determination to serve Him. Make the decision to be the light that Jesus has called you to be, regardless of the opinions of others. Looking to Elijah as an example, determine to stand before the children of spiritual Israel as the Lord directs, confident that He will turn the hearts of His people back to Him, using your steadfast light as a beacon to point the way.

Noah:
When God's Directions
Make No Sense

THE STRUGGLE

We are, by nature, rational beings. When faced with a dilemma, we try to work things through in our mind, make sense of circumstances, and form a logical solution. Often, our endeavors are unsuccessful. The predicament we face typically unravels, but not in a way that we had considered. However, a lifetime of failed attempts does not derail us – every new situation offers a challenge to our psyche, and the cycle continues.

As Christians, we learn to take our dilemmas to the Lord, seeking His help. We know that "all things work together for good to them that love God, to them who are the called according to His purpose" (Romans 8:28). We apply our faith, because He teaches us to "ask in faith, nothing wavering. For he that wavereth is like a wave of the sea driven with the wind and tossed. For let not that man think that he shall receive any thing of the Lord" (James 1:6-7).We desire to know His wisdom and to follow His ways. Frequently the Lord will instruct us in what He would have us to do. At times, however, His instructions seem to make no sense.

The enemy of our soul often uses these times to birth doubt within us. In the Garden of Eden, Satan wielded this same weapon against Eve. "Ye shall not surely die: For God doth know that in the day ye eat thereof, then your eyes shall be opened, and ye shall be as gods, knowing good and evil." (See Genesis 2: 1-5) Eve perceived that the fruit was good – it appealed to the lust of the eyes, the lust of the flesh, and the pride of life. Considering the fruit's goodness, why would God withhold it from them? Thus, the seed of doubt was planted, and we, as the sons and daughters of Eve, have tried to fit the Lord's ways into the box of our own understanding ever since.

THE STORY
GENESIS 6:13-8:19

God spoke with Noah, revealing that He intended to destroy all flesh by sending a flood. He told Noah to build an ark, giving explicit instructions regarding its design. Noah built the ark and filled it with all manner of food. He, his family, and pairs of every animal entered the ark, and the flood began. It rained relentlessly for forty days and forty nights. Noah, his family, and the animals remained on the ark for one year and ten days.

THE RELEVANCE

When Noah first heard God's instructions, I am sure his mind teemed with questions. Would his family believe that the Lord had told him to build an ark? How long would the rain last? Would the ark be adequate to keep him and his family safe? How would he gather enough food and supplies to provide for his family and the animals? What would they do if the supplies ran out too soon? Furthermore, would God really destroy all living creatures? Noah and his family had sinned, as well. Why had God chosen to spare them? Would God allow him to bring his friends and neighbors on the ark also? Would this act of judgment conquer the evilness of man's heart? If Noah's future generations walked in sin and disobedience, would God again bring destruction?

Despite the many questions racing through Noah's mind, he had a choice to make – trust the words of the Lord or disregard them. Noah chose to believe the words of God, and began building the ark according to the instructions the Lord had given him. That is not the end of the story, however. It would have taken Noah years to build the ark. During that time, what was the reaction of the community? Did Noah warn them of the judgment to come? They had already rejected Noah's teachings (see 2 Peter 2:6), as well as the prophecy of Enoch (see Jude 14-15). We can presume that Noah had to endure their ridicule and scorn while he built the ark. When Noah and his family boarded the ark and the rains began, I am sure public opinion suddenly changed. We can easily imagine hundreds, perhaps even thousands, of people scrambling to climb aboard the ark, not out of repentance but out of fear. I wonder if Noah, on the other side of the door, could hear the townspeople calling his name. How hard it must have been to have to ignore their pleas, knowing that the Lord's judgment had come and that they, because of unbelief and unrepentant hearts, would perish!

As Noah and his family rode out the storm safely tucked away in the ark, they had plenty of time to meditate on the words of the Lord and the events that had occurred. Noah knew they had done nothing to deserve God's mercy. When He sent judgment, it could have included Noah and his family, as well. They loved the Lord, but they were not perfect. No, the only reason God had chosen to save them was mercy. They loved God; therefore, He chose to show them favor.

Despite favor, Noah still had to choose. What would have happened if Noah had not believed God – if he had not built the ark? I can almost feel Noah's mind jolt as it stumbled onto this realization. What a fine line between life and death! One choice would pave the way – to a cruise and a fresh beginning, or to perishing with the rest of the world.

Isaiah 55:8-9 says, "For my thoughts are not your thoughts, neither are your ways my ways, saith the Lord. For as the heavens are higher than the earth, so are my ways higher than your ways, and my thoughts than your thoughts." One thing that lures us to God is His mysteriousness. It appeals to us and draws us to Him. He is always doing something to surprise us.

Do not "grow up" so much that you try to understand the Lord's thoughts and ways. Learning a magician's tricks takes much of the delight out of watching the trick as it is performed. In the same way, we can lose some of the fervor and passion in our relationship with the Lord if He fits into our understanding. Instead, learn to enjoy the mystery that He is. Rather than attempting to decipher why He tells you to do something, do it with delight, anticipating finding out His purpose in His timing. In the meantime, look to Noah and remember the consequences of one choice.

5

Peter:
When Plagued by Guilt

THE STRUGGLE

When we first come to Christ, it is solely on His promise to "forgive us our sins and to cleanse us from all unrighteousness" (1 John 1:9). As we continue to walk with Him, we know that His mercies are new every morning (see Lamentations 3:22-23). We stumble and fall, yet His word assures us of His grace and love, even in our weaknesses and failures. At times, however, Satan attempts to blind us to the Lord's mercy. He obstructs our vision until all we can see are the mistakes we have made. We feel tormented by guilt. This shame often hinders our relationship with the Lord. We believe that we have messed up so much that He no longer loves or desires us.

THE STORY
MARK 14:26-31; MARK 14:66-72; JOHN 21:15-17

Jesus foretold that the disciples would be offended by Him. Peter refuted Jesus' prophecy, stating that though everyone else may be offended, he would not. Jesus replied that Peter would deny Him three times before the cock crowed twice. Peter intensified his denial.

Within the next few hours, Judas betrayed Jesus, the fearful disciples fled, and Jesus stood on trial for His life. Peter had returned but remained at a distance. The high priest's maid recognized Peter, but Peter claimed he did not understand what she said. He went out to the porch, and a cock crowed. There, another servant noticed him and said, "He is one of them." Peter denied it a second time. Soon after, the bystanders noted his Galilean accent and agreed that he must be one of Jesus' followers. Peter vehemently denied their claims. Immediately the cock crowed a second time, and Peter recalled Jesus' prophecy.

THE RELEVANCE

Can you imagine Peter's state of mind after the cock crowed the second time? When he remembered Christ's words, he wept. The word "wept" is *klaio*, meaning, "to wail aloud." This kind of crying indicates heart-wrenching remorse. I imagine that as Peter wept, he thought back over the past few hours. Jesus had warned Peter of what would happen, but Peter did not listen. If he had heeded Jesus' words and been attentive, perhaps he could have altered the outcome. Looking back, Peter could recognize that his denial was a manifold offense; he had insulted the other disciples by implying that Jesus' prediction was true for them but not for himself. He relied on his zeal for Jesus to overcome fear, rather than acknowledging his own fleshly weaknesses. Furthermore, his denial insinuated that Jesus could lie, that His words could not be trusted.

Over the next several days, Peter's guilt is still evident. Twice we find him, along with the remaining disciples, gathered behind locked doors out of fear. John 20 reveals that John and Peter beheld the empty tomb and believed

Mary's story, yet they did not truly believe that Jesus had risen, as evidenced in verse 9. In John 21:3, Peter decided to go fishing, with several other disciples joining him. This verse indicates that they were fishing, not for pleasure, but for income. This had been their manner of living before Jesus called them. Now He was gone, but they were still responsible for providing for their families.

If it is to be noticed, all of the disciples were troubled, not just Peter. They all wrestled with the pain of losing their beloved Jesus; they all struggled with the stories of His resurrection. They all huddled behind locked doors out of fear, and at least half of them returned to their old lifestyles.

What makes Peter stand out? How was he any different from the others?

Just like the disciples, situations can occasionally arise in our own lives that cause us to experience fear, doubt, or shame. Typically, we are able to recognize the negative feeling, and prayerfully give it over to God, allowing Him to remove it from us. At times, however, the emotion may seem to loom larger and stronger than normal, and we feel powerless in its grasp. I believe that was the case for Peter. He repented, but he could not forgive himself, and his shame weighed heavily on his heart. However, although Peter did not realize it at the time, Jesus was singling him out for a divine appointment with mercy.

In Mark 16, Mary Magdalene, Mary the mother of James, and Salome had come to anoint Jesus' body. Instead, they encountered an angel, who told them of Jesus' resurrection. The angel instructed the women to convey a message to "His disciples and Peter." They were to travel to Galilee, where Jesus would come to them. They made the journey, but it appears that their outlook had not changed. Once in Galilee, Peter went fishing, reverting to the ways he had known before Jesus. Six other disciples joined him. Although they were in Galilee according to the angel's instructions, their focus was physical and not spiritual. Their concern was not to seek out Jesus, but rather to return to providing for their families.

While the disciples were in the boat fishing, a man on the shore spoke with them. When

Peter learned that it was Jesus, he left the disciples behind, swimming quickly to the shore. Powerful emotions lead to powerful actions. Generally, the more intensely we feel something, the more intensely we react to it. For the past few days, Peter, along with the rest of the disciples, had been fearful, regretful, and despondent. They had seen the risen Jesus at least twice, and while I am sure the disciples were amazed and relieved, Scriptures do not reveal joy of any kind. However, with the disciples in the boat and Jesus on the shore, we see a change come over Peter. He could not get to his Lord fast enough. The six disciples remained in the boat, struggling with the net full of fish, but Peter's focus was entirely on Jesus.

If you are struggling with feelings of guilt and shame, the first priority must be to adjust your focus. If you look inward, you can see the emotions that threaten to choke you. If you look directly in front of you, you can see the net, bursting at the seams with fish. This is your livelihood, your income and provision for your family. However, can you look beyond the net? There, in the distance stands a Man.

Do you recognize Him for who He is? Within you, the emotions still exist. They have not become extinct simply because you caught a glimpse of Jesus. Before you, your long-awaited opportunity lies at your feet, finally within your grasp. Yet, when you turn your eyes to the shore, you sense a longing that emotions cannot quench and financial gain cannot fulfill.

Desperate and unwilling to wait a moment longer, Peter left the safety and comfort of the boat, leapt into the water, and swam to the shore. A glimpse of Jesus is not enough to heal the broken heart. Jesus tells us in Matthew 11:28, "Come unto me, all you who labor and are heavy laden, and I will give you rest." Notice Jesus does not say He will come to us; He instructs us to come to Him.

In John 21:15-17, Jesus and the disciples enjoyed a meal together. Afterwards, Jesus addresses Peter, asking three times, "Do you love me?" Each time, Peter answered in the affirmative, to which Jesus responded with instructions to feed His sheep.

In verses 16 and 17, Jesus asks Peter, "Do you love me?" Peter replies, "Yes, Lord; You know that I love You." Jesus uses the word *agapao*, which means, "to love in a social or moral sense"; it refers to a devoted and absolute love. Peter responds with the word *phileo*, meaning, "to be a friend of; to have affection for." The two are similar, but *agapao* refers primarily to an emotion of the heart, while *phileo* refers primarily to a choice of the mind. In verse 17, Jesus asks Peter a third time, "Do you love me?" This time, however, He uses the same word *phileo*. I believe this is the cause of Peter's distress. He perceived that Jesus lessened His question; He no longer asked for an absolute love from the heart, but a willful choice of the mind.

This passage holds an amazing lesson for us today. Jeremiah 17:9 reveals, "The heart is deceitful above all things, and desperately wicked: who can know it?" Our emotions are constantly changing, and can lead us in the wrong direction. How many couples have divorced because the love that once held them together dissolved over time? The feelings of our heart cannot be trusted. God loves us with an *agapao* love – He is completely devoted to us, and his love for us is absolute. Can we honestly declare that our love for Him is the same? Could Peter? If Peter had loved Jesus with an *agapao* love, he would not have denied Him. Likewise, if we were capable of a devoted and absolute love, we would never fail Him. However, the truth is that we, like Peter, do fail Him at times.

If that were the end of the story, we would be a hopeless and condemned people. Yet Jesus did not stop there. He asked Peter a third time; yet this time He used the word *phileo*, pertaining to a choice of the mind. Often, you may feel love for God springing up from a fountain within you; it is easy to follow Him then. Conversely, when your best friend and mentor is dying, everyone you trusted has fled, and the whole town is seeking your life, the heart is in no condition to make lead you. Following your heart in that moment would most likely lead you to deny your Lord. However, following your mind in that moment would entail making a decision based on beliefs and choices you have previously made. Peter had previously made the choice to follow Jesus. Over the next few years, he repeatedly made choices that reflected his allegiance to Jesus. When Jesus asked, "Do you love me?" for the third time, He was asking for Peter's continued allegiance. He was asking whether Peter would choose to love Him with His mind, determining to follow Him, despite emotions that may enter his heart.

Revelation 12:10 tells us that Satan stands before God day and night to accuse us. He informs God of our weaknesses and failures, attempting to place us under condemnation and judgment. Remember, however, that Satan is a liar. Our weaknesses and failures may be very real; yet Romans 8:1 reveals, "There is therefore now no condemnation to them which are in Christ Jesus, who walk not after the flesh, but after the Spirit." When you feel weighed down by guilt or shame, read again the story of Peter's denial and subsequent redemption. As you do so, remember:

- Repent. God will not remove feelings of guilt if you are still guilty. "If we confess our sins, He is faithful and just to forgive us our sins, and to cleanse us from all unrighteousness." (1 John 1:9)

- Look beyond the turmoil inside of you and the circumstances in front of you, and notice the Man standing in the distance beckoning you.

- Recognize that the decision is yours – you can stay in the comfort of the boat and pray that He comes to you, or you can jump out of the boat and determine that nothing will deter you from reaching Him.

- Be aware that time and circumstances can alter the emotions of the heart. Even when feelings of guilt, shame, fear, or unbelief overpower the love you feel for God, realize that love is an action. You have already chosen to follow Christ, and over the years have made many choices that reflect your choice. Decide now to continue following Him, confident that as you draw near to Him and spend time in His presence, He will vanquish those deceitful feelings.

Esther:
Courage in the
Midst of Fear

THE STRUGGLE

On our Christian journey, we do not have to travel very far before discovering that God expects us to leave our comfort zones. No matter what calling He has placed on our lives, it can cause fear to rise up within us. It's not that we are unwilling to do as He asks; we are simply waiting for Him to give us the boldness to do it. Most ministers have experienced this struggle. They recognize the call to preach, and even though they love the Lord and desire to do His will, most of them end up running from the call for months or even years. In most cases, the primary reason is fear. Whether it's fear of speaking in front of people, fear of failure, or fear of what people will think, these men and women become bound by their fear. At worst, these men and women turn from God completely, because they become so lost in the struggle that they feel powerless to escape. At best, they spend months or years telling the Lord, "If You help me conquer this fear, I will then submit to Your calling on my life."

THE STORY
ESTHER 3-4

King Ahasuerus promoted a man by the name of Haman, and set him above all the princes. According to the king's command, all were to bow and reverence Haman, showing honor to his position.

Mordecai, a man of Jewish descent and an employee of the king's government, did not bow to Haman. Upon questioning, Mordecai explained that as a Jew, he could not bow to man, but only to his God. Haman became infuriated. However, rather than take his anger out on Mordecai alone, he decided to kill all of the Jews. He approached King Ahasuerus with the information that the Jews did not obey the king's laws, and that they should be destroyed. King Ahasuerus permitted Haman to do what seemed right to the Jews. Haman chose a particular day for every Jew to be killed, and sent notices, sealed with the king's seal, to every province.

When Mordecai learned of Haman's intent and decree, he spoke with Esther through messengers. At first, Esther's response was that she could do nothing about the decree. Approaching the king unbidden meant probable death, and the king had not shown Esther any sign of favor recently. Mordecai reminded Esther that, although he was confident that God would send a deliverer from elsewhere, she was a Jew, and therefore would be killed along with her family. Esther requested that Mordecai and the Jews hold a three-day fast, and she and her maidens inside the palace would do the same. She would then go to the king, despite the danger.

THE RELEVANCE

I've heard it said that desperate times call for desperate measures. I believe this adage bears true for Esther. From her viewpoint, she was doomed either way. If she did not speak with the king and convince him to change the decree, she would die, along with all of her people. If she did go to the king, she faced death anyway, possibly before even having a chance to plead her cause.

The first thing that is vital to observe in this story is the three-day fast. Remember that Esther was born a Jew. Known as Hadassah, she was raised with the knowledge of God and His covenant with the Jewish people. Coupling Esther 2:16 with 3:7, we learn that Esther had been queen for five years when the decree was made. For five years, Hadassah had hidden her heritage, and was known as Esther. During this time, she would have had to keep her faith in the one true God secret, and would have been regularly subjected to false idols.

Once Esther learned of the decree, we witness a resurfacing of her faith in God. She did not choose to keep silent about God, nor did she appeal to the idols that were so popular. Instead, her immediate action was to call a fast, petitioning God for assistance.

Matthew 26:41 tells us that "...The spirit indeed is willing, but the flesh is weak." Making the commitment to go before the king did not lessen Esther's fear. Read Esther 4:16 again. "Go, gather together all the Jews who are present in Shushan, and fast ye for me, and neither eat not drink three days, night or day: I also and my maidens will fast likewise; and so will I go in unto the king, which is not according to the law: and if I perish, I perish." Notice the purpose of the fast – "Fast for me." She did not ask the Israelites to fast for God's protection in battle, or for the decree to be rescinded. She asked them to fast for *her*. In essence, Esther tells Mordecai, "I am committed. I will attempt to liberate our people from this decree. However, my life will be in danger. I am terrified. My life is in God's hands; if I die, so be it. This one thing I ask. Have all the Jews fast and pray for me. I need strength and courage to do this."

Esther is an Old Testament role model for every modern-day believer. Her response provides us with a road map when our own journey becomes an obstacle course of fear.

First, we must ensure where our faith lies. In Chapter one, we learned the importance of our faith being placed properly in the cross of Christ. No matter what situation we face today that causes fear to rise, we must understand that the blood Christ shed on the cross purchased us. Satan no longer has a legal hold on us. Because we now belong to God, we are joint-heirs with Christ. Everything that belongs to Christ belongs to us, as well. Christ has overcome the world, the flesh, and the devil. Likewise, by constantly looking to what He did for us on the cross, we are able to overcome the world, the flesh, and the devil. For Esther, this meant overcoming Haman's plan to kill the Jews, her own fears, and Satan's plan to destroy the lineage that Christ would come through.

Second, we must commit to doing the will of the Father, despite our own personal emotions or the unknown outcome of the situation. God knows when we are fearful, yet He still calls us to action. He expects us to place Him as our highest priority, seeking to fulfill every plan He has for us. We are not to suspend our obedience to Him simply because fear surfaces. I have heard of preachers who, after many years of preaching, still become physically ill when they are scheduled to minister before a congregation. Yet they remain faithful to the calling God has placed on their lives. As my former pastor once said, "Do it afraid, but do it anyway."

Finally, although we are not to give in to our feelings, we cannot ignore them, either. For us to put on a brave face and say we have no fear is to lie. The Lord knows our thoughts and our emotions. How can I expect God to heal me of a sickness if I do not admit that I am sick and need to be healed? Likewise, He will not heal our fears if we simply ignore them. We must be able to examine our hearts, be honest in what we feel, and trust those emotions to God. During this process, it is advisable to enlist the help of fellow believers. Esther asked her people to fast for her. James 5:16 says, "Confess your faults one to another, and pray one for another, that you may be healed. The effectual fervent prayer of a righteous man avails much." This Scripture refers mainly to areas of weakness or struggle. There is power in numbers. If we are struggling to gain victory in a particular area, it helps to know that others are praying for us. God, in His ultimate wisdom, created us that way, and then urged us to "Bear ye one another's burdens, and so fulfill the law of Christ" (Galatians 6:2). Furthermore, Matthew 18:19 reminds us, "Again I say unto you, That if two of you shall agree on earth as touching any thing that they shall ask, it shall be done for them of my Father which is in Heaven."

7

Abraham:
When The Cost
Seems Too High

THE STRUGGLE

Luke 14:28-30 tells of a man building a tower. Before beginning construction, the man first sits down and figures out how the expense of building the tower, and whether he has enough to afford it. In the spiritual sense, this passage informs us that we must count the cost of being Christ's follower.

Matthew 10:34-39 tells us that even our own family must not be more important to us than Christ. If we place anything or anyone above Christ, then we are not worthy of Him.

The question, then, is what price are we willing to pay? Have we sat down and counted the cost of following Christ? Conversely, have we drawn lines in the sand, informing the Lord by our attitudes or actions that there are limits to our love towards Him?

In theory, we recognize that Christ is to have the utmost position in our hearts. We acknowledge that we are not to place anyone or anything above Him. In theory, we readily agree to follow Him, despite all cost.

In reality, however, we often come to a standstill in our Christian walk because of difficulties or situations that arise. Friends become distant, claiming that we take this "Jesus-stuff" too seriously. Family members ridicule us for preaching to them. Co-workers are perplexed when we won't lie on our performance reviews in order to advance our career. Our feelings of frustration and betrayal mount. Over time we find ourselves asking God why we have lost our friends, why our marriage has lost its joy, why we lost out on the promotion although we are well qualified.

How should we cope with these very real feelings of loss? What cost can we expect to pay for a relationship with Christ? Haven't we been taught that salvation is freely given?

THE STORY
GENESIS 12; 13; 15; 17; 21

The story of Abraham begins in Genesis 12. God told Abraham to leave his family and his home, and that He would make of him a great nation. We find in verse 4 that Abraham was at this time seventy five years old. After Abraham had reached the plain of Moreh, the Lord told Abraham that He would give the land to Abraham's seed. In Genesis 13, Abraham returned to Canaan, and he and Lot separated. The Lord again promised to raise up children to Abraham, and to give the land to his seed.

Chapter 15 opens with the Lord comforting a fearful Abraham, saying, "I am your shield, and your exceeding great reward." Abraham asked, "What will you give me, seeing I am childless? You have not given me children, and a servant shall be my heir." The Lord responded by again promising to raise up seed to Abraham.

In chapter 16, Abraham laid with Hagar, his wife's handmaid. Hagar conceived, and gave birth to a son, Ishmael. At this time, Abraham was eighty six years old.

In chapter 17, the Lord reaffirmed the promise to make nations from Abraham, and revealed the terms of the covenant that is to be between the Lord, Abraham, and Abraham's seed. He informed Abraham that Ishmael would be blessed, but that the covenant would be established with Isaac, whom Sarah would bear the following year.

Chapter 21 illustrates the birth of Isaac, the casting out of Hagar and Ishmael by Sarah, and the provision and protection of Ishmael by the Lord. Abraham was now one hundred years old.

In Genesis 22, God told Abraham to take Isaac and offer him as a sacrifice. Abraham took Isaac to a mountain, bound him, and laid him upon the wood. He then unsheathed his knife and prepared to slay his son. However, the angel of the Lord called to Abraham, and instructed him to not harm Isaac, for Abraham had proven his faithfulness to God. Looking up, Abraham found a ram caught in a bush, and offered it for a sacrifice instead.

THE RELEVANCE

This is a difficult chapter to write, and even more difficult to accept. I would like to tell you that being a Christian means never having to lose; that nothing you hold dear will ever be taken from you. I would like to tell you that. But it would be a lie.

Being a follower of Christ does not mean that life is never hard. It simply means we have someone walking with us on our journey, someone who understands, sympathizes, and gives us the strength we need to endure.

The truth is, we will encounter loss at times. We will be called to give up things or people that we love. Like Jacob, we may lose health or physical ability. Mary had to risk losing, not only her own reputation, but Joseph's, as well. Repeatedly, Paul was placed in prison, losing his freedom. As Abraham, we may even be called to give up our children.

As individuals, we view our relationship with Christ from our own viewpoint. It is often helpful, however, to view the relationship from His viewpoint. This is easier to do for those who are parents.

God is our Father. He cares for us in the same way that we care for our own children. Toddlers are known for putting everything in their mouth. As a toddler, your child may pick up a pen and begin chewing on it. As a parent, you know there is nothing wrong with that pen. It is a good thing, and can be very useful. However, you also understand that your toddler is not mature enough to use the pen properly. Although the pen is a helpful instrument, in your toddler's hand it can be become a dangerous item. Because of this, you take the pen from him. You are not trying to be mean; you are trying to protect him. Furthermore, you are not implying that he can never have a pen; you are simply saying that he may have the pen when he is mature enough to use it properly.

In the same way, we often desire things of this world, or even particular gifts of the Spirit, and cannot understand why we cannot have them. We may feel like we have to give up our desires and dreams in order to please the Lord. At times, He may call us to allow our dreams and goals to line up with His own. However, His Word also promises that He will give us the desires of our heart. If my desire lines up with His will for my life, then I can be assured that He will give me the desire of my heart. I may not have the fulfillment of that desire yet, but I can understand, from a parental point of view, that He is waiting until I am mature enough to possess the object of my desire safely and purposefully.

Because He is a good Father, God also cares about who we allow to influence us. Our children may befriend someone who causes us worry or concern. We may, at times, have to inform our child that she is not allowed to be around a particular person. More than likely, she will become angry with us; she does not understand why we are trying to control her. However, we can see farther into the future than she can. She only sees the fun she has with this friend now. We, on the other hand, can foresee the friend influencing our child with a negative attitude or bad habits.

Likewise, our hearts hurt when friends begin distancing themselves from us because of our faith. We may, on occasion, recognize that the Lord is leading us to distance ourselves from others, as well. From our own viewpoint, we see the best in our friends. We know there may be a few negative behaviors, yet we rationalize this by hoping that we will be able to witness and change our friend. God, however, sees that the negative behaviors of our friend is, in reality, influencing us. We are to be a light to the world, and to witness to those in our lives, but we must be careful who we are closely associated with, as well.

There are times when the cost seems too high. We cannot see the purpose in having to give up certain things or people. For one battling a life-threatening disease, it can be difficult to understand why God would allow this. A person who has been wrongly accused of a crime may lose their freedom by being placed in prison, or lose their reputation in the community. The parent whose child is prostituting herself to support her drug habit may feel that their child has been taken from them. In these circumstances, the feelings of loss can be unbearable. We often come to a point of believing the cost is too high. We feel like we have given up more than we can bear.

These emotions are very real, and they are very raw. I cannot tell you how to erase them. I can only attempt to give you a different viewpoint, and teach you how to use the Word of God to combat the emotions.

The one facing a life-threatening disease must believe that God is still in the healing business. Our humanistic viewpoint sees our health deteriorating. However, God sees the end result. Depending on His purpose, He will give you either a glorious testimony of how He healed you from this debilitating illness, or a glorified body that will be forever in His presence and that will never feel sickness or pain again.

The one wrongly accused of a crime must believe that God is our vengeance. He knows our deeds. Everything that is done in darkness will be brought to light. In His timing, and in His way, you will be vindicated. The Lord also warns us to not come against His anointed.

Those who come against you will be brought to judgment by God, and your name will be cleared. Remember, Psalm 23 says that He prepares a table before us *in the presence* of our enemies. He doesn't always remove our enemies. Controversially, He sometimes keeps our enemies around us while He is blessing us, that our enemies will see the hand of God upon us. By this, you will gain favor with man, and possibly a few converts to the glory of God.

The parent of the child who has gone astray and is lost to the world must believe that God is able to protect and reach our child even when we cannot. If we have raised that child in the ways of the Lord, we can hold to His promise that she will not depart from it when she is old, despite the circumstances we see now. If we are children of God, we can believe and proclaim that we *and our household* shall be saved. As the prodigal son eventually returned to his father, you will regain your child, who, in turn, may be able to witness to others who are in the same path of destruction.

Knowing the Word of God will not change any situation we face. We must *believe* the Word of God. 2 Corinthians 5:7 says, "For we walk by faith, not by sight." Where does our belief lie? In the circumstances we see in the natural, or in the supernatural power of God to fulfill all that He has spoken?

The Lord allows loss in our lives. However, it is always with a purpose. As with Abraham, if we are faithful to give up what the Lord asks of us, He will always provide us with something wonderfully different.

CONCLUSION

The Bible teaches us that God has emotions. He displays love, hate, joy, jealousy, and sadness. We are created in His image. Therefore, we are emotional beings. Our purpose is not to defeat our emotions, but to ensure that they line up with God's emotions. We have learned that the heart is deceitful, and wicked above all things. Rather than letting our emotions control us, we are to control our emotions. Instead of attempting to bottle up our feelings and putting on a robotic mask, our emotions should be portrayed, but in the proper context. Rather than displaying hatred towards one who has wronged us, we are to display a hatred towards sin. Instead of having jealousy in our marriage, we are to have jealousy in our relationship with the Lord.

In the beginning of this book, I referred to our walk with Christ as a battle. Paul confirms this.

> *Finally, my brethren, be strong in the Lord, and in the power of His might. Put on the whole armor of God, that you may be able to stand against the wiles of the devil. For we wrestle not against flesh and blood, but against principalities, against powers, against the rules of the darkness of this world, against spiritual wickedness in high places. Wherefore take unto you the whole armor of God, that you may be able to withstand in the evil day, and having done all, to stand. Stand therefore, having your loins gird about with truth, and having on the breastplate of righteousness; and your feet shod with the preparation of the gospel of peace; above all, taking the shield of faith, wherewith you shall be able to quench all the fiery darts of the wicked. And take the helmet of salvation, and the*

sword of the Spirit, which is the Word of God. – Ephesians 6:10-17

The power of the Lord's might was displayed through the death of Christ on the cross. His blood paid the penalty of sin for us. Through this sacrifice, Satan's hold over us was broken. He will attempt to come against us, but Jesus has already won the victory. For us to be victorious in our own lives, we must ever look to Jesus, placing our faith in what He has done for us

Notice in the above passage that we are not in a offensive position. We are not told to wage an attack against Satan. Rather, we are to be on the defense. We are to stand, which refers to not giving ground, no matter how hard our enemy comes against us.

We are to stand with our loins girt about with truth. The loin is the thigh. That is where our strength to stand lies; it is our balance. If we are standing on a lie, the ground is not stable, and we can easily be toppled. The truth of God's Word is unchangeable; if we are standing on His truth, we cannot fall.

We are to put on the breastplate of righteousness. The breastplate covers our torso, including our heart. Our righteousness comes from Christ and His sacrifice on the cross. We have no righteousness within ourselves. As we put on Christ's righteousness, we are choosing to let our hearts and emotions be led by His heart and His emotions.

Our feet are to be shod with the preparation of the gospel of peace. Our feet refer to our walk with the Lord. The gospel of peace is the Word of God; it is the message that man can have peace with God, but only through the cross of Christ. Notice, however, the word "preparation." We cannot share the gospel of peace unless we have prepared. This means we must be studying the Word of God. In this Ephesians passage, our feet are not walking, but standing. If we are to effectively "stand against the wiles of the devil," then we must be prepared by knowing God's Word.

We are further told to take "the shield of faith, wherewith [we] shall be able to quench all the fiery darts of the wicked." As previously stated, the Word of God is powerless in our lives unless we *believe* it. I am to study the Scriptures in order to know and understand them; I must then apply my faith, believing that God will do what He said He will do. Then, when the wicked one comes against me, my shield of faith protects the darts from piercing me.

We are to put on the helmet of salvation. As the breastplate covers the heart, the helmet covers the mind. Ephesians 4:23 refers to being renewed in the spirit of our mind. This refers to understanding that everything we receive from God is because of what Christ did for us at Calvary. Because of His sacrifice, I am a child of God. Because I am His child, I can be assured of His love and concern for me. As a good Father, He will come to my rescue, no matter what threat arises. Jesus died on the cross to save me, and I place my faith in His victory over the flesh, the world, and the devil. As a result, God the Father fights for me. I can be encouraged in the understanding that when God is on my side, then all of Heaven defends me.

The final element of our armor is the sword of the Spirit, which is the Word of God. Because I am a child of God, every word in the Bible applies to me and my circumstances. No matter what situation I face, I can know that the Word of God is my weapon. With this Word, I am able to defend myself against every attack of the enemy. I am able to defeat his purposes for me. In the wilderness, Satan came against Jesus several times, but Jesus defeated him by using the Word of God. We can do the same.